TRAFFIC SECRETES

A PROVEN LIST BUILDING METHOD TO GET MORE THAN 1000 SUBSCRIBERS IN 30DAYS

WILFRED JOHN

© 2023

Table of Contents

Chapter 1: 7

Understanding Internet Traffic 7

Basics 7

Chapter 2: 13

Measuring 13

And Analyzing Online 13

Traffic 13

Chapter: 3 19

SEO Strategies for Driving 19

Traffic to Your Website 19

Here are some general strategies that can be used to drive traffic to a website through SEO 23

Chapter 4: 25

Paid Advertising for 25

Traffic Generation 25

Chapter 5: 33

Content Marketing for Attracting 33

Online Visitors 33

Chapter 6: 39

Social Media Marketing for Increasing 39

Website Traffic 39

Chapter 7: 45

Influencer Marketing for Boosting 45

Online Traffic 45

Chapter 8: 51

Email Marketing for Driving Traffic 51

To Your Website 51

Chapter 9: 56

Affiliate Marketing for Generating 56

Traffic and Sales 56

Chapter 10: 61

Video Marketing for Attracting 61

Online Viewers 61

Chapter 11: 66

Podcasting for Generating Traffic and Building an Audience
.... 66

Chapter 12: 72

Forum Marketing for Attracting 72

Targeted Traffic 72

Chapter 13: 77

Blogging for Driving Traffic and 77

Engaging Readers 77

Chapter 14: 82

Slideshare and Other Presentation Sharing Sites for
Generating Traffic 82

Chapter 15: 87

Local SEO for Attracting Local 87

Traffic to Your Business 87

Chapter 16: 93

International SEO for Attracting 93

Global Traffic 93

Chapter 17: 99

E-commerce Traffic Strategies 99

For Online Stores 99

Chapter 18: 104

Mobile Marketing for Reaching Mobile Users 104

Chapter 19: 109

App Marketing for Driving Traffic to 109

Mobile Apps 109

Chapter 20: 115

Online Public Relations for Generating Traffic and Building Visibility 115

Chapter 21: 120

Online Reputation Management for Protecting and Enhancing Traffic 120

Chapter 22: 123

Web Design and User Experience for Boosting Traffic and Conversions 123

Chapter 23: 128

Conversion Optimization for Turning 128

Traffic into Customers 128

Chapter 24: 137

Analyzing and Improving Your Online Traffic Mix 137

Chapter 25: 141

Advanced Strategies for Maximizing Your Online Traffic Potential 141

Chapter 1: Understanding Internet Traffic Basics

Understanding Internet traffic is essential for anyone looking to optimize their online presence. In this chapter, we will delve into the basics of Internet traffic and explore how it works, how it is measured, and how it can be analyzed.

First, let's define Internet traffic. Simply put, Internet traffic refers to the data that is transmitted over the Internet. This can include anything from website content and emails to video streams and social media updates. When you visit a website, your computer or device sends a request to the server hosting that website, and the server responds by sending back the requested data. This exchange of data is what is known as Internet traffic.

There are several ways to measure Internet traffic, including page views, unique visitors, and time spent on a website. Page views refer to the number of times a page on a website has been viewed. Unique visitors, on the other hand, are the number of individual people who have visited a website. Time spent on a website is a measure of how long a visitor stays on a site. These metrics can be useful for understanding the popularity and engagement of a website.

It's important to note that not all Internet traffic is equal. There are different types of traffic that can have a different impact on a website. For example, direct traffic refers to visitors who type a website's URL directly into their browser. Referral traffic refers to visitors who arrive at a website through a link on another site. Search traffic refers to visitors who arrive at a website through a search engine. Each of these types of traffic can have a different value and importance for a website.

Another aspect of Internet traffic to consider is its source. Traffic can come from various sources, such as search engines, social media, and email marketing. Understanding the source of your traffic can help you identify which marketing efforts are most effective and where to focus your efforts.

Analyzing Internet traffic is crucial for understanding how well a website is performing. There are a variety of tools available for analyzing traffic, such as Google Analytics. These tools can provide insights into where visitors are coming from, what pages they are visiting, and how long they are staying on a site. This information can help website owners make informed decisions about how to optimize their site for better performance.

In addition to understanding the basics of Internet traffic, it's also important to consider the impact of traffic on a website's performance. A high volume of traffic can be a good thing, but it can also put a strain on a website's server and lead to slow loading times or even crashes.

To ensure that a website can handle a large volume of traffic, it's important to properly size the server and infrastructure. This can involve investing in more powerful hardware, such as faster processors and more memory, or using cloud-based solutions to scale up as needed. It's also important to optimize the website itself to ensure that it is performing as efficiently as possible. This can involve optimizing images and other media, minifying code, and using caching techniques to reduce the load on the server.

In addition to technical considerations, it's also important to consider the impact of traffic on the user experience. A website that is slow to load or difficult to navigate can drive visitors away, even if it has a high volume of traffic. To ensure that visitors have a positive experience, it's important to optimize the website for usability and accessibility. This can involve using responsive design techniques to ensure that the website looks good on any device, and ensuring that the website is easy to navigate and use.

Finally, it's worth considering the impact of traffic on the overall online ecosystem. As more people come online and more devices connect to the Internet, the demand for bandwidth and other resources is increasing. Ensuring that traffic is managed in a responsible and sustainable way can help to ensure that the Internet remains a viable and valuable resource for everyone.

In conclusion, understanding Internet traffic is essential for anyone looking to succeed online. By understanding how traffic works, how it is measured, and how it can be analyzed, you can make informed decisions about how to drive traffic to your website and how to optimize your site for the best possible performance. By considering the impact of traffic on a website's performance, the user experience, and the overall online ecosystem, you can ensure that your online efforts are sustainable and effective.

Chapter 2: Measuring And Analyzing Online Traffic

Measuring and analyzing online traffic is an essential part of optimizing a website or online presence. By understanding how traffic is behaving, website owners and marketers can make informed decisions about how to improve performance and achieve their goals. In this chapter, we will explore the various ways to measure and analyze online traffic, and discuss the tools and techniques that can be used to do so.

One of the most basic ways to measure online traffic is through page views. Page views refer to the number of times a page on a website has been viewed. This metric can be useful for understanding the popularity and engagement of a website, as well as for identifying which pages are performing well and which may need improvement.

Unique visitors is another important metric for measuring online traffic. Unique visitors refer to the number of individual people who have visited a website. This metric can be useful for understanding the reach and audience of a website, as well as for identifying patterns in visitor behavior.

Time spent on a website is another metric that can be used to measure online traffic. This metric reflects how long a visitor stays on a site and can be useful for understanding engagement and interest in a website's content.

In addition to these basic metrics, there are a variety of other ways to measure and analyze online traffic. For example, it's important to consider the source of traffic, such as whether it is coming from search engines, social media, or referral sources. Understanding the source of traffic can help website owners and marketers understand the effectiveness of their marketing efforts and where to focus their efforts.

There are also a variety of tools available for measuring and analyzing online traffic. Google Analytics is a popular tool that provides a wealth of data and insights about website traffic, including the source of traffic, the pages visited, and the duration of visits. Other tools, such as website heat maps and session replay tools can provide more detailed insights into how visitors are interacting with a website.

In addition to using tools and metrics to measure and analyze traffic, it's also important to consider the overall performance and user experience of a website. This can involve analyzing metrics such as loading times, bounce rates, and conversion rates. By understanding how these metrics are performing, website owners and marketers can identify areas for improvement and optimize their website for better performance.

There are a few key things to keep in mind when measuring and analyzing online traffic. First, it's important to set clear goals and objectives for your website or online presence. This will help you determine what metrics are most relevant and important to track, and will provide a benchmark against which to measure your progress.

It's also important to regularly review and analyze your traffic data. This will help you identify trends and patterns, and will allow you to make informed decisions about how to optimize your website or online presence.

Another key consideration is to ensure that your traffic measurement and analysis tools are set up correctly. This may involve installing tracking code on your website, configuring your analytics tools, and setting up goals and conversions. By taking the time to properly set up your measurement and analysis tools, you can ensure that you are getting accurate and reliable data.

In addition to tracking and analyzing your own traffic, it can also be helpful to compare your traffic data to industry benchmarks and standards. This can provide a sense of how your website or online presence is performing relative to others in your industry, and can help you identify areas for improvement.

Finally, it's important to remember that traffic measurement and analysis is an ongoing process. As your website or online presence evolves, your traffic patterns and behavior will change. It's important to regularly review and analyze your traffic data to ensure that you are making the most of your online presence.

It's also worth noting that there are several privacy considerations to keep in mind when measuring and analyzing online traffic. With the increasing use of tracking technologies such as cookies and pixels, it's important to be transparent about how you are collecting and using data and to ensure that you are in compliance with relevant laws and regulations such as the General Data Protection Regulation (GDPR) and the California Consumer Privacy Act (CCPA).

To protect user privacy, it's important to provide clear and concise information about how you are using tracking technologies and to give users the option to opt out of tracking if they so choose. It's also important to ensure that any data you collect is used for legitimate business purposes and is not shared or sold to third parties without the user's consent.

In addition to compliance with laws and regulations, it's also important to consider the ethical implications of tracking and analyzing online traffic. It's essential to be transparent and upfront about your data collection and use practices, and to respect users' privacy and autonomy.

By being mindful of privacy considerations when measuring and analyzing online traffic, you can build trust with your users and ensure that your online presence is compliant and ethical.

Finally, it's important to remember that traffic measurement and analysis is an ongoing process. As your website or online presence evolves, your traffic patterns and behavior will change. It's important to regularly review and analyze your traffic data to ensure that you are making the most of your online presence.

In conclusion, measuring and analyzing online traffic is an important part of optimizing a website or online presence, but it's essential to be mindful of privacy considerations. By being transparent about your data collection and use practices and complying with relevant laws and regulations, you can build trust with your users and ensure that your online presence is compliant and ethical.

Chapter: 3
SEO Strategies for Driving Traffic to Your Website

Search engine optimization (SEO) is the process of optimizing a website in order to improve its visibility and ranking in search engine results pages (SERPs). By optimizing a website for relevant keywords and phrases, businesses and organizations can attract more qualified traffic to their site and increase their visibility online. In this chapter, we will explore the various SEO strategies that can be used to drive traffic to a website.

One key aspect of SEO is keyword research and selection. Identifying the keywords and phrases that are most relevant to your business and target audience can help you optimize your website for those terms and attract more qualified traffic. There are a variety of tools available for keyword research, including Google's Keyword Planner and SEM rush.

Another key aspect of SEO is on-page optimization. This involves optimizing the content and structure of your website in order to make it more visible and relevant to search engines. This can include optimizing title tags, Meta descriptions, headings, and other elements of your website's code and content.

Off-page optimization is another important aspect of SEO. This refers to the activities that take place outside of your own website that can impact its visibility and ranking in search engine results. This can include building high-quality back links from other reputable websites, as well as leveraging social media and other online platforms to build visibility and credibility.

In addition to these core SEO strategies, there are a few other considerations to keep in mind when optimizing a website for search engines. For example, it's important to ensure that your website is mobile-friendly and that it loads quickly, as both of these factors can impact its ranking in search engine results. It's also important to consider the user experience of your website and to ensure that it is easy to navigate and use.

Finally, it's important to track and measure the results of your SEO efforts in order to understand the effectiveness of your strategies and to identify areas for improvement. Tools such as Google Analytics can provide valuable insights into your traffic and performance, and can help you understand how your SEO efforts are paying off.

There are a few key best practices to keep in mind when implementing SEO strategies to drive traffic to your website. First, it's important to focus on creating high-quality, informative, and engaging content that is relevant to your target audience. By producing valuable content that meets the needs and interests of your audience, you can attract more qualified traffic and improve your visibility in search engine results.

Another best practice is to ensure that your website is technically sound and that it follows best practices for search engine optimization. This can include ensuring that your website is mobile-friendly, that it loads quickly, and that it is easy to navigate. It can also involve optimizing your website's code and structure to make it more visible and crawl able to search engines.

It's also important to regularly review and update your SEO strategies in order to stay current and to adapt to changes in search engine algorithms and user behavior. This can involve conducting keyword research, analyzing your website's performance, and identifying areas for improvement.

In addition to these best practices, it's important to be mindful of the ethical and legal considerations involved in SEO. This can include avoiding spammy or manipulative tactics, and ensuring that you are in compliance with relevant laws and regulations such as the General Data Protection Regulation (GDPR) and the California Consumer Privacy Act (CCPA).

By following these best practices and being mindful of ethical and legal considerations, you can effectively drive traffic to your website through SEO and improve your online visibility.

Here are some general strategies that can be used to drive traffic to a website through SEO:

1. Keyword research: Identifying the most relevant and popular keywords for the website and including them in the content and metadata (such as the title tags and headings).
2. On-page optimization: Ensuring that the website is well-organized, easy to navigate, and free of technical errors that could impact search engine crawling and indexing.
3. Content creation: Developing and publishing high-quality, original content that provides value to the website's target audience and includes the targeted keywords.
4. Link building: Obtaining links from other high-quality, authoritative websites back to the website. These links can help to improve the website's visibility and credibility in the eyes of search engines.
5. Local SEO: Optimizing the website for local search by including location-specific information and ensuring that the website is listed in local business directories and on map listings.

6. Mobile optimization: Ensuring that the website is mobile-friendly and performs well on mobile devices, as more and more users are accessing the web from their phones and tablets.

In conclusion, there are a few key best practices to keep in mind when implementing SEO strategies to drive traffic to your website. By focusing on high-quality content, ensuring that your website is technically sound and optimized, and regularly reviewing and updating your strategies, you can effectively drive traffic to your website and improve your online visibility. By being mindful of ethical and legal considerations, you can ensure that your SEO efforts are sustainable and effective.

Chapter 4: Paid Advertising for Traffic Generation

Paid advertising is a powerful tool for generating traffic to a website or online presence. By purchasing ads on platforms such as Google Ad Words, Facebook, or LinkedIn, businesses and organizations can reach a targeted audience and drive traffic to their site. In this chapter, we will explore the various forms of paid advertising and discuss the benefits and considerations of using paid ads for traffic generation.

One of the most common forms of paid advertising is pay-per-click (PPC) advertising. With PPC advertising, businesses and organizations pay a fee each time an ad is clicked. This can be a highly effective way to drive targeted traffic to a website, as ads can be targeted to specific keywords and demographics. Google Ad Words is the most popular platform for PPC advertising, but there are also other platforms such as Bing Ads and Yahoo Gemini.

Another form of paid advertising is display advertising. With display advertising, businesses and organizations purchase ad space on websites or other online platforms and pay a fee based on the number of impressions (how many times the ad is displayed) or clicks the ad receives. This can be a useful way to increase brand awareness and drive traffic to a website.

Social media advertising is another popular form of paid advertising. By purchasing ads on platforms such as Facebook, Instagram, and LinkedIn, businesses and organizations can reach a targeted audience and drive traffic to their site. Social media advertising can be particularly effective for reaching a specific demographic or for promoting content or events.

In addition to these forms of paid advertising, there are also other options such as native advertising and sponsored content. Native advertising involves placing ads in a format that is similar to the surrounding content, and is often used to promote content or products. Sponsored content refers to content that is paid for by a business or organization and is typically marked as sponsored or paid for.

There are several benefits to using paid advertising for traffic generation. One key benefit is the ability to reach a targeted audience. By carefully selecting the keywords, demographics, and platforms for your ads, you can ensure that your ads are being seen by the people most likely to be interested in your products or services. Paid advertising can also be a quick and effective way to drive traffic to a website. Unlike organic traffic, which can take time to build up, paid ads can start generating traffic almost immediately. This can be particularly useful for businesses and organizations that need to generate traffic quickly, such as for a promotional event or product launch.

Another benefit of paid advertising is the ability to track and measure the results of your campaigns. Most paid advertising platforms provide detailed analytics and reporting tools that allow you to track the performance of your ads and understand how they are impacting your traffic and performance. This can help you optimize your campaigns and make informed decisions about how to allocate your advertising budget.

There are a few key considerations to keep in mind when using paid advertising for traffic generation. One is the cost of advertising. While paid advertising can be an effective way to drive traffic, it can also be expensive, particularly for highly competitive keywords or industries. It's important to carefully consider your budget and to make sure that your advertising costs are justified by the results you are achieving.

Another consideration is the need to constantly optimize and adjust your campaigns. In order to get the most out of your paid advertising efforts, it's important to regularly review and optimize your campaigns to ensure that they are performing as effectively as possible. This can involve adjusting your targeting, ad copy, and budget to get the best results.

There are several different factors to consider when planning and implementing a paid advertising campaign for traffic generation. One key factor is the type of ad you want to run. As mentioned earlier, there are several different types of paid advertising, including pay-per-click (PPC) ads, display ads, social media ads, native ads, and sponsored content. Each type of ad has its own benefits and considerations, and it's important to choose the right type of ad for your specific goals and audience.

Another key factor to consider is the platform on which you will run your ads. There are many different platforms available, including Google Ad Words, Bing Ads, Yahoo Gemini, Facebook, Instagram, and LinkedIn. Each platform has its own unique features and capabilities, and it's important to choose the platform that is best suited to your needs and goals.

Another factor to consider is your target audience. It's important to have a clear understanding of who you are trying to reach with your ads and to tailor your targeting accordingly. This can involve selecting specific keywords, demographics, or interests to target, as well as choosing the right platforms and ad formats to reach your audience.

It's also important to consider the budget for your paid advertising campaign. This will involve setting a budget for your ad spend and determining how to allocate your budget across different ad formats and platforms. It's important to carefully track and measure the results of your campaigns to ensure that you are getting the best return on your investment.

Finally, it's important to consider the messaging and creative elements of your ads. This includes the ad copy, images, and overall design of your ads, as well as the call to action that you are using to encourage users to click on your ads. It's important to create compelling and effective ads that will grab the attention of your target audience and encourage them to take action.

There are a few best practices to keep in mind when using paid advertising for traffic generation. One key best practice is to set clear goals and objectives for your campaigns. This will help you determine the right ad formats, platforms, and targeting to use, and will provide a benchmark against which to measure the success of your campaigns.

Another best practice is to conduct thorough keyword research and to use relevant and targeted keywords in your ad copy and targeting. By using the right keywords, you can ensure that your ads are being seen by the people most likely to be interested in your products or services.

It's also important to create compelling and effective ad copy and design. This includes crafting a clear and compelling call to action and using images and other design elements that will grab the attention of your target audience.

It's also crucial to track and measure the results of your paid advertising campaigns. By using analytics and reporting tools provided by the platform on which you are running your ads, you can understand how your campaigns are performing and identify areas for improvement.

Finally, it's important to be mindful of ethical and legal considerations when using paid advertising. This includes following the terms of service of the platforms on which you are running your ads, as well as complying with relevant laws and regulations such as the General Data Protection Regulation (GDPR) and the California Consumer Privacy Act (CCPA).

By following these best practices and being mindful of ethical and legal considerations, you can effectively use paid advertising to drive traffic to your website or online presence and achieve your goals.

In conclusion, there are a few key best practices to keep in mind when using paid advertising for traffic generation. These include setting clear goals and objectives, conducting thorough keyword research, creating compelling and effective ad copy and design, tracking and measuring the results of your campaigns, and being mindful of ethical and legal considerations. By following these best practices, you can effectively use paid advertising to drive traffic to your website or online presence and achieve your goals.

Chapter 5: Content Marketing for Attracting Online Visitors

Content marketing is a strategy that involves creating and sharing valuable, relevant, and consistent content in order to attract and retain a clearly defined audience. By providing valuable and informative content, businesses and organizations can attract and retain customers, and drive traffic to their website or online presence. In this chapter, we will explore the various forms of content marketing and discuss the benefits and considerations of using content marketing for attracting online visitors.

One key aspect of content marketing is content creation. This can involve creating a range of content types such as blog posts, articles, videos, podcasts, infographics, and more. It's important to create content that is valuable, informative, and relevant to your target audience and to the goals of your content marketing efforts.

Another important aspect of content marketing is content distribution. This involves sharing your content on a variety of platforms and channels in order to reach and engage your target audience. This can include your own website or blog, as well as social media platforms, email marketing, and other online channels.

One of the key benefits of content marketing is the ability to build credibility and trust with your audience. By providing valuable and informative content, you can establish yourself as a thought leader in your industry and build trust with your audience. This can lead to increased engagement and loyalty from your audience and can drive traffic to your website or online presence.

Another benefit of content marketing is the ability to drive conversions and sales. By providing valuable content that addresses the needs and interests of your target audience, you can encourage your audience to take action, whether that be signing up for a newsletter, making a purchase, or engaging with your brand in some other way.

In addition to these benefits, content marketing can also help you to improve your search engine ranking and drive organic traffic to your website. By creating high-quality and relevant content, you can improve your visibility in search engine results and attract more qualified traffic to your site.

There are a few key considerations to keep in mind when using content marketing to attract online visitors. One is the need to create high-quality and relevant content. It's important to understand the needs and interests of your target audience and to create content that meets those needs and interests. It's also important to ensure that your content is well-written, informative, and engaging.

Another consideration is the need to have a clear content marketing strategy. This will involve setting clear goals and objectives for your content marketing efforts, identifying your target audience, and determining the types of content you will create and the channels you will use to share your content. It's also important to have a plan for measuring and tracking the performance of your content marketing efforts in order to understand what is working and what can be improved.

In addition to these considerations, it's important to be mindful of ethical and legal considerations when using content marketing. This can include ensuring that your content is accurate and truthful, and complying with relevant laws and regulations such as the General Data Protection Regulation (GDPR) and the California Consumer Privacy Act (CCPA).

By following these best practices and being mindful of ethical and legal considerations, you can effectively use content marketing to attract online visitors and drive traffic to your website or online presence.

There are several different types of content that can be used as part of a content marketing strategy. Some common types of content include:

- Blog posts: Blog posts are a popular form of content that can be used to share information, ideas, and insights with an audience. Blog posts

can be written in a variety of styles and can cover a wide range of topics.
- Articles: Articles are longer-form pieces of content that are typically more in-depth and informative than blog posts. Articles can be published on a variety of platforms, including websites, magazines, and online publications.
- Videos: Video content is a popular and effective way to share information and engage an audience. Videos can be used to demonstrate products, explain concepts, or provide entertainment.
- Podcasts: Podcasts are audio recordings that can be listened to on demand. Podcasts can be a great way to share information and ideas with an audience in an engaging and convenient format.
- Info graphics: Info graphics are visual representations of information and data that can be used to explain complex concepts or ideas in an easy-to-understand format.
- Social media posts: Social media platforms such as Facebook, Instagram, and Twitter are a great way to share content and engage with an audience. By sharing valuable and informative content on social media, businesses and organizations can drive traffic to their website or online presence and build a following.

By using a variety of content types, businesses and organizations can reach and engage their target audience in a way that is most effective for their goals and needs.

In conclusion, there are several different types of content that can be used as part of a content marketing strategy. These include blog posts, articles, videos, podcasts, info graphics, and social media posts. By using a variety of content types, businesses and organizations can reach and engage their target audience in a way that is most effective for their goals and needs.

Chapter 6:
Social Media Marketing for Increasing Website Traffic

Social media marketing is the process of using social media platforms to promote a product, service, or brand, and to drive traffic to a website or online presence. By creating and sharing valuable, relevant, and engaging content on social media, businesses and organizations can build relationships with their audience, increase brand awareness, and drive traffic to their website or online presence. In this chapter, we will explore the various forms of social media marketing and discuss the benefits and considerations of using social media for increasing website traffic.

One key aspect of social media marketing is content creation. This involves creating and sharing valuable, relevant, and engaging content on social media platforms in order to attract and retain a clearly defined audience. This can include a variety of content types such as text, images, videos, infographics, and more.

Another important aspect of social media marketing is engagement. This involves actively interacting with your audience on social media platforms in order to build relationships and foster a sense of community. This can involve responding to comments, answering questions, and sharing user-generated content.

One of the key benefits of social media marketing is the ability to reach a large and targeted audience. With billions of users on platforms such as Facebook, Instagram, and Twitter, businesses and organizations can reach a wide audience and target their marketing efforts to specific demographics and interests.

Another benefit of social media marketing is the ability to drive traffic to a website or online presence. By sharing links to your website or other online properties on social media, you can drive traffic and increase visibility for your business or organization.

In addition to these benefits, social media marketing can also help to improve search engine ranking and drive organic traffic to a website. By creating and sharing high-quality and relevant content on social media, businesses and organizations can improve their visibility in search engine results and attract more qualified traffic to their site.

There are a few key considerations to keep in mind when using social media marketing to increase website traffic. One is the need to create high-quality and relevant content. It's important to understand the needs and interests of your target audience and to create content that meets those needs and interests. It's also important to ensure that your content is well-written, informative, and engaging.

Another consideration is the need to have a clear social media marketing strategy. This will involve setting clear goals and objectives for your social media efforts, identifying your target audience, and determining the types of content you will create and the platforms you will use to share your content. It's also important to have a plan for measuring and tracking the performance of your social media marketing efforts in order to understand what is working and what can be improved.

In addition to these considerations, it's important to be mindful of ethical and legal

considerations when using social media marketing. This can include ensuring that your content is accurate and truthful, and complying with relevant laws and regulations such as the General Data Protection Regulation (GDPR) and the California Consumer Privacy Act (CCPA).

By following these best practices and being mindful of ethical and legal considerations, you can effectively use social media marketing to increase website traffic and achieve your goals.

There are several different social media platforms that businesses and organizations can use as part of their social media marketing efforts. Some of the most popular platforms include:

- Facebook: Facebook is the largest social media platform with over 2.7 billion monthly active users. Businesses and organizations can create a Facebook page and share content, engage with followers, and run ads to reach a targeted audience.
- Instagram: Instagram is a visual social media platform with over 1 billion monthly active

users. Businesses and organizations can create an Instagram account and share photos, videos, and other visual content, as well as engage with followers and run ads.
- Twitter: Twitter is a micro blogging platform with over 330 million monthly active users. Businesses and organizations can create a Twitter account and share short messages, or "tweets," as well as engage with followers and run ads.
- LinkedIn: LinkedIn is a professional networking platform with over 690 million users. Businesses and organizations can create a LinkedIn company page and share content, engage with followers, and run ads to reach a professional audience.
- Pinterest: Pinterest is a visual platform that allows users to "pin" images and other visual content to virtual boards. Businesses and organizations can create a Pinterest account and share images and other visual content, as well as run ads to reach a targeted audience.

By using a combination of these platforms, businesses and organizations can reach a wide and targeted audience and drive traffic to their website or online presence.

In conclusion, social media marketing is a powerful tool for increasing website traffic and driving visibility for a business or organization. By creating and sharing valuable, relevant, and engaging content on social media platforms, businesses and organizations can build relationships with their audience, increase brand awareness, and drive traffic to their website or online presence. By creating high-quality and relevant content, having a clear social media marketing strategy, and being mindful of ethical and legal considerations, you can effectively use social media marketing to increase website traffic and achieve your goals.

Chapter 7: Influencer Marketing for Boosting Online Traffic

Influencer marketing is a type of marketing that involves partnering with individuals who have a large and engaged following on social media or other online platforms. By working with these influencers, businesses and organizations can reach a large and targeted audience and drive traffic to their website or online presence. In this chapter, we will explore the various forms of influencer marketing and discuss the benefits and considerations of using influencer marketing for boosting online traffic.

One key aspect of influencer marketing is identifying the right influencers to work with. This involves finding individuals who have a large and engaged following that is relevant to your business or organization, and who align with your brand values and messaging.

Another important aspect of influencer marketing is negotiating and executing the partnership. This can involve determining the terms of the partnership, such as the type of content that will be created, the payment or compensation for the influencer, and any performance metrics that will be used to measure the success of the partnership.

One of the key benefits of influencer marketing is the ability to reach a large and targeted audience. By working with influencers who have a large and engaged following, businesses and organizations can reach a wide audience and target their marketing efforts to specific demographics and interests.

Another benefit of influencer marketing is the ability to drive traffic to a website or online presence. By partnering with influencers who share links to your website or other online properties, you can drive traffic and increase visibility for your business or organization.

In addition to these benefits, influencer marketing can also help to improve brand awareness and credibility. By working with influencers who are respected and trusted by their followers, businesses and organizations can build credibility and trust with their audience.

There are a few key considerations to keep in mind when using influencer marketing to boost online traffic. One is the need to carefully research and select the right influencers to work with. It's important to find influencers who have a large and engaged following that is relevant to your business or organization, and who align with your brand values and messaging.

Another consideration is the need to have a clear influencer marketing strategy. This will involve setting clear goals and objectives for your influencer marketing efforts, identifying the right influencers to work with, and determining the terms of the partnership. It's also important to have a plan for measuring and tracking the performance of your influencer marketing efforts in order to understand what is working and what can be improved.

In addition to these considerations, it's important to be mindful of ethical and legal considerations when using influencer marketing. This can include ensuring that partnerships are disclosed in accordance with relevant laws and regulations, and that influencers are accurately representing your brand and products or services

It's also important to be transparent and honest in your communications with influencers and to respect their needs and boundaries.

By following these best practices and being mindful of ethical and legal considerations, you can effectively use influencer marketing to boost online traffic and achieve your goals.

There are several different ways that businesses and organizations can work with influencers as part of their marketing efforts. Some common forms of influencer marketing include:

- Sponsored posts: Sponsored posts involve influencers sharing content about a product, service, or brand on their social media or other online platforms. This can include sharing a review, demonstration, or other information about the product or service, and including a link to the business's website or online presence.
- Affiliate marketing: Affiliate marketing involves influencers promoting a product or service and earning a commission for any sales that result

from their promotion. This can involve sharing a special link or discount code with their followers that can be used to make a purchase.
- Collaborations: Collaborations involve influencers and businesses or organizations working together to create content that promotes a product, service, or brand. This can involve creating a sponsored video or blog post, or hosting a giveaway or other promotion.
- Brand ambassadorships: Brand ambassadorships involve influencers promoting a product, service, or brand on an ongoing basis. This can involve sharing content about the product or service, engaging with followers, and representing the brand at events or other promotional activities.

By using a combination of these approaches, businesses and organizations can effectively work with influencers and drive traffic to their website or online presence.

In conclusion, influencer marketing is a powerful tool for boosting online traffic and driving visibility for a business or organization. By partnering with individuals who have a large and engaged following, businesses and organizations can reach a wide and targeted audience and drive traffic to their website or online presence. By carefully researching and selecting the right influencers, having a clear influencer marketing strategy, and being mindful of ethical and legal considerations, you can effectively use influencer marketing to boost online traffic and achieve your goals.

Chapter 8: Email Marketing for Driving Traffic To Your Website

Email marketing is a strategy that involves using email to promote a product, service, or brand, and to drive traffic to a website or online presence. By sending targeted and engaging emails to a subscribed list of individuals, businesses and organizations can build relationships with their audience, increase brand awareness, and drive traffic to their website or online presence. In this chapter, we will explore the various forms of email marketing and discuss the benefits and considerations of using email marketing for driving traffic to your website.

One key aspect of email marketing is building and maintaining an email list. This involves collecting the email addresses of individuals who are interested in receiving emails from your business or organization. This can be done through a variety of methods such as opt-in forms on your website, sign-up sheets at events, or by offering incentives for subscribing to your email list.

Another important aspect of email marketing is creating and sending emails. This involves creating engaging and targeted emails that are designed to promote a product, service, or brand, and to drive traffic to a website or online presence. It's important to create emails that are well-written, informative, and visually appealing, and to send emails at a frequency that is appropriate for your audience.

One of the key benefits of email marketing is the ability to reach a large and targeted audience. By building and maintaining an email list, businesses and organizations can reach a wide audience and target their marketing efforts to specific demographics and interests.

Another benefit of email marketing is the ability to drive traffic to a website or online presence. By including links to your website or other online properties in your emails, you can drive traffic and increase visibility for your business or organization.

In addition to these benefits, email marketing can also help to improve brand awareness and credibility. By regularly sending engaging and valuable emails to your subscribers, you can build credibility and trust with your audience.

There are a few key considerations to keep in mind when using email marketing to drive traffic to your website. One is the need to build and maintain a high-quality email list. It's important to collect the email addresses of individuals who are interested in receiving emails from your business or organization and to ensure that you have permission to send emails to these individuals.

Another consideration is the need to create high-quality and targeted emails. It's important to understand the needs and interests of your audience and to create emails that meet those needs and interests. It's also important to ensure that your emails are well-written, informative, and visually appealing.

In addition to these considerations, it's important to be mindful of ethical and legal considerations when using email marketing. This can include ensuring that you have permission to send emails to individuals, and complying with relevant laws and regulations such as the General Data Protection Regulation (GDPR) and the CAN-SPAM Act.

There are several different types of emails that businesses and organizations can send as part of their email marketing efforts. Some common types of emails include:

- Newsletters: Newsletters are regular emails that are sent to subscribers and include updates, news, and other information about a business or organization.
- Promotional emails: Promotional emails are designed to promote a specific product, service, or event, and typically include a call-to-action to encourage the reader to take a specific action, such as making a purchase or visiting a website.
- Transactional emails: Transactional emails are emails that are triggered by a specific action, such as a purchase or sign-up. These emails can include receipts, confirmation emails, and other types of information that are relevant to the specific action.
- Abandoned cart emails: Abandoned cart emails are sent to customers who have added items to their online shopping cart but have not

completed the purchase. These emails can be used to remind customers of their items and encourage them to complete their purchase.

By using a combination of these types of emails, businesses and organizations can effectively use email marketing to drive traffic to their website or online presence.

In conclusion, email marketing is a powerful tool for driving traffic to a website or online presence. By building and maintaining an email list and sending targeted and engaging emails, businesses and organizations can build relationships with their audience, increase brand awareness, and drive traffic to their website or online presence. By building a high-quality email list, creating targeted and high-quality emails, and being mindful of ethical and legal considerations, you can effectively use email marketing to drive traffic to your website and achieve your goals.

Chapter 9: Affiliate Marketing for Generating Traffic and Sales

Affiliate marketing is a type of performance-based marketing in which a business or organization rewards affiliates for each visitor or customer brought to the business by the affiliate's own marketing efforts. By working with affiliates who promote your products or services, you can drive traffic and sales to your website or online presence. In this chapter, we will explore the various forms of affiliate marketing and discuss the benefits and considerations of using affiliate marketing for generating traffic and sales.

One key aspect of affiliate marketing is selecting the right affiliates to work with. This involves finding individuals or organizations who have a large and engaged following and who align with your brand values and messaging. It's also important to consider the type of products or services that the affiliates will be promoting, as well as the type of audience they are targeting.

Another important aspect of affiliate marketing is establishing the terms of the partnership. This can involve determining the commissions that affiliates will receive, as well as any performance metrics that will be used to measure the success of the partnership.

One of the key benefits of affiliate marketing is the ability to reach a large and targeted audience. By working with affiliates who have a large and engaged following, businesses and organizations can reach a wide audience and target their marketing efforts to specific demographics and interests.

Another benefit of affiliate marketing is the ability to drive traffic and sales to a website or online presence. By partnering with affiliates who promote your products or services and include links to your website or other online properties, you can drive traffic and increase sales for your business or organization.

In addition to these benefits, affiliate marketing can also help to improve brand awareness and credibility. By working with affiliates who are respected and trusted by their followers, businesses and organizations can build credibility and trust with their audience.

There are a few key considerations to keep in mind when using affiliate marketing to generate traffic and sales. One is the need to carefully research and select the right affiliates to work with. It's important to find affiliates who have a large and engaged following and who align with your brand values and messaging. It's also important to consider the type of products or services that the affiliates will be promoting, as well as the type of audience they are targeting.

Another consideration is the need to have a clear affiliate marketing strategy. This will involve setting clear goals and objectives for your affiliate marketing efforts, identifying the right affiliates to work with, and determining the terms of the partnership. It's also important to have a plan for measuring and tracking the performance of your affiliate marketing efforts in order to understand what is working and what can be improved.

In addition to these considerations, it's important to be mindful of ethical and legal considerations when using affiliate marketing.

This can include ensuring that partnerships are disclosed in accordance with relevant laws and regulations, and that affiliates are accurately representing your brand and products or services.

There are several different ways that businesses and organizations can work with affiliates as part of their marketing efforts. Some common forms of affiliate marketing include:

- Affiliate links: Affiliate links are special tracking links that affiliates use to promote a product or service. When a visitor clicks on the affiliate link and makes a purchase, the affiliate earns a commission.
- Affiliate banners: Affiliate banners are banner ads that affiliates can display on their website or other online platform. When a visitor clicks on the banner and makes a purchase, the affiliate earns a commission.
- Affiliate programs: Affiliate programs are structured programs that allow affiliates to promote a business or organization's products or services in exchange for a commission. Affiliate programs often include tools and

resources to help affiliates promote the products or services effectively.

By using a combination of these approaches, businesses and organizations can effectively work with affiliates and generate traffic and sales for their website or online presence.

In conclusion, affiliate marketing is a powerful tool for generating traffic and sales for a business or organization. By working with affiliates who promote your products or services and include links to your website or other online properties, you can drive traffic and increase sales for your business or organization. By carefully researching and selecting the right affiliates, having a clear affiliate marketing strategy, and being mindful of ethical and legal considerations, you can effectively use affiliate marketing to generate traffic and sales and achieve your goals.

Chapter 10: Video Marketing for Attracting Online Viewers

Video marketing is a strategy that involves using video content to promote a product, service, or brand, and to attract online viewers. By creating and sharing engaging and informative video content, businesses and organizations can increase brand awareness, drive traffic to their website or online presence, and convert viewers into customers. In this chapter, we will explore the various forms of video marketing and discuss the benefits and considerations of using video marketing for attracting online viewers.

One key aspect of video marketing is creating high-quality and engaging video content. This involves developing a clear concept and message for the video, and ensuring that the video is visually appealing and professionally produced. It's also important to consider the length and format of the video, as well as the target audience and the platform on which the video will be shared.

Another important aspect of video marketing is promoting and distributing the video. This can involve sharing the video on social media and other online platforms, as well as using paid advertising to reach a wider audience. It's also important to optimize the video for search engines by including relevant keywords and tags, and to track and analyze the performance of the video.

One of the key benefits of video marketing is the ability to attract a large and engaged audience. By creating high-quality and engaging video content, businesses and organizations can capture the attention of their audience and keep them engaged.

Another benefit of video marketing is the ability to drive traffic to a website or online presence. By including links to your website or other online properties in the video or in the video's description, you can drive traffic and increase visibility for your business or organization.

In addition to these benefits, video marketing can also help to improve brand awareness and credibility. By creating professional and informative video content, businesses and organizations can build credibility and trust with their audience.

There are a few key considerations to keep in mind when using video marketing to attract online viewers. One is the need to create high-quality and engaging video content. It's important to develop a clear concept and message for the video, and to ensure that the video is visually appealing and professionally produced. It's also important to consider the length and format of the video, as well as the target audience and the platform on which the video will be shared.

Another consideration is the need to effectively promote and distribute the video. This will involve sharing the video on social media and other online platforms, and using paid advertising to reach a wider audience. It's also important to optimize the video for search engines and to track and analyze the performance of the video.

In addition to these considerations, it's important to be mindful of ethical and legal considerations when using video marketing. This can include ensuring that you have permission to use any images or music in the video, and complying with relevant laws and regulations such as copyright laws.

There are several different types of videos that businesses and organizations can create and share as part of their video marketing efforts. Some common types of videos include:

- Product videos: Product videos are designed to showcase a specific product or service and can include demonstrations, reviews, or other information about the product or service.
- Explainer videos: Explainer videos are designed to explain a concept, product, or service in an engaging and easy-to-understand way. These videos can be helpful for introducing a new product or service to a broad audience.
- How-to videos: How-to videos are designed to provide step-by-step instructions on how to do something. These videos can be helpful for teaching viewers a new skill or providing them with information on how to use a product or service.
- Testimonial videos: Testimonial videos are designed to showcase the experiences of real customers or clients using a product or service.

These videos can help to build credibility and trust with potential customers.

In conclusion, video marketing is a powerful tool for attracting online viewers and driving traffic to a website or online presence. By creating high-quality and engaging video content and promoting and distributing the video effectively, businesses and organizations can increase brand awareness, drive traffic, and convert viewers into customers. By creating professional and informative video content, promoting and distributing the video effectively, and being mindful of ethical and legal considerations, you can effectively use video marketing to attract online viewers and achieve your goals.

Chapter 11: Podcasting for Generating Traffic and Building an Audience

Podcasting is a form of digital media that involves creating and sharing audio content, typically in the form of a series of episodic programs. By creating and sharing engaging and informative audio content, businesses and organizations can increase brand awareness, drive traffic to their website or online presence, and build an engaged and loyal audience. In this chapter, we will explore the various forms of podcasting and discuss the benefits and considerations of using podcasting for generating traffic and building an audience.

One key aspect of podcasting is creating high-quality and engaging audio content. This involves developing a clear concept and message for the podcast, and ensuring that the audio is professionally produced and easy to listen to. It's also important to consider the format of the podcast, as well as the target audience and the platform on which the podcast will be shared.

Another important aspect of podcasting is promoting and distributing the podcast. This can involve sharing the podcast on social media and other online platforms, as well as using paid advertising to reach a wider audience. It's also important to optimize the podcast for search engines by including relevant keywords and tags, and to track and analyze the performance of the podcast.

One of the key benefits of podcasting is the ability to build an engaged and loyal audience. By creating high-quality and engaging audio content and consistently releasing new episodes, businesses and organizations can attract and retain a dedicated group of listeners.

Another benefit of podcasting is the ability to drive traffic to a website or online presence. By including links to your website or other online properties in the podcast or in the podcast's description, you can drive traffic and increase visibility for your business or organization.

In addition to these benefits, podcasting can also help to improve brand awareness and credibility. By creating professional and informative audio content, businesses and organizations can build credibility and trust with their audience.

There are a few key considerations to keep in mind when using podcasting to generate traffic and build an audience. One is the need to create high-quality and engaging audio content. It's important to develop a clear concept and message for the podcast, and to ensure that the audio is professionally produced and easy to listen to. It's also important to consider the format of the podcast, as well as the target audience and the platform on which the podcast will be shared.

Another consideration is the need to effectively promote and distribute the podcast. This will involve sharing the podcast on social media and other online platforms, and using paid advertising to reach a wider audience. It's also important to optimize the podcast for search engines and to track and analyze the performance of the podcast.

In addition to these considerations, it's important to be mindful of ethical and legal considerations when using podcasting. This can include ensuring that you have permission to use any images or music in the podcast, and complying with relevant laws and regulations such as copyright laws.

There are many different types of podcasts, covering a wide range of topics and formats. Here are a few examples:

1. News and current affairs podcasts: These podcasts cover news and current events, and may include interviews with experts and analysis of current issues.
2. Educational podcasts: These podcasts are designed to teach listeners about a particular subject or topic. They may include lectures, interviews with experts, and discussions of research and studies.
3. Interview podcasts: These podcasts typically feature interviews with guests, who may be experts in a particular field or simply interesting people with a story to tell.
4. Narrative podcasts: These podcasts tell a story over the course of multiple episodes. They may be fiction or non-fiction, and may be based on real events or entirely fictional.

5. Comedy podcasts: These podcasts are designed to be entertaining and humorous, and may include stand-up comedy routines, sketch comedy, or comedic interviews and discussions.
6. Sports podcasts: These podcasts cover a wide range of sports-related topics, including analysis of games and events, interviews with players and coaches, and discussion of current issues in the world of sports.
7. True crime podcasts: These podcasts explore real-life crime cases, often in great detail and with a focus on the investigative process.
8. Business and entrepreneurship podcasts: These podcasts cover topics related to business and entrepreneurship, including interviews with successful businesspeople, advice on starting and growing a business, and discussion of current trends and issues.

In conclusion, podcasting is a powerful tool for generating traffic and building an engaged and loyal audience. By creating high-quality and engaging audio content and promoting and distributing the podcast effectively, businesses and organizations can increase brand awareness, drive traffic, and build a dedicated group of listeners. By creating professional and informative audio content, promoting and distributing the podcast effectively, and being mindful of ethical and legal considerations, you can effectively use podcasting to generate traffic and build an audience and achieve your goals.

Chapter 12: Forum Marketing for Attracting Targeted Traffic

Forum marketing is a strategy that involves participating in online forums or discussion groups related to your industry or niche, with the goal of attracting targeted traffic to your website or online presence. By actively participating in these forums and sharing valuable and relevant information, businesses and organizations can build credibility, establish themselves as thought leaders, and drive traffic to their website or online presence. In this chapter, we will explore the various forms of forum marketing and discuss the benefits and considerations of using forum marketing for attracting targeted traffic.

One key aspect of forum marketing is finding and participating in relevant forums or discussion groups. This involves researching and identifying forums or discussion groups related to your industry or niche, and actively participating in these forums by starting and contributing to discussions, answering questions, and providing valuable and relevant information. It's important to be authentic and transparent in your forum participation, and to avoid spamming or self-promotion.

Another important aspect of forum marketing is tracking and analyzing your forum participation. This involves using tools and analytics to measure the effectiveness of your forum marketing efforts, and to understand what is working and what can be improved. It's also important to monitor your online reputation and respond to any negative feedback or comments in a professional and constructive manner.

One of the key benefits of forum marketing is the ability to attract targeted traffic to your website or online presence. By actively participating in relevant forums and sharing valuable and relevant information, you can drive traffic to your website or online presence and increase visibility for your business or organization.

Another benefit of forum marketing is the opportunity to build credibility and establish yourself as a thought leader in your industry or niche. By consistently providing valuable and relevant information and participating in discussions, you can build credibility and trust with your target audience.

There are a few key considerations to keep in mind when using forum marketing to attract targeted traffic. One is the need to find and participate in relevant forums or discussion groups. It's important to research and identify forums or discussion groups related to your industry or niche, and to actively participate in these forums by starting and contributing to discussions, answering questions, and providing valuable and relevant information.

Another consideration is the need to track and analyze your forum participation. This will involve using tools and analytics to measure the effectiveness of your forum marketing efforts, and to understand what is working and what can be improved. It's also important to monitor your online reputation and respond to any negative feedback or comments in a professional and constructive manner.

In addition to these considerations, it's important to be mindful of ethical and legal

considerations when using forum marketing. This can include ensuring that you are complying with the terms of service of the forums or discussion groups you are participating in, and being respectful of other users and their opinions.

There are several different types of forums or discussion groups that businesses and organizations can participate in as part of their forum marketing efforts. Some common types of forums include:

- Industry-specific forums: Industry-specific forums are forums or discussion groups that are focused on a specific industry or niche. These forums can be helpful for connecting with other professionals and industry experts in your field, and for sharing knowledge and insights.
- General interest forums: General interest forums are forums or discussion groups that cover a wide range of topics and are not specific to any particular industry or niche. These forums can be helpful for connecting with a broad audience and for sharing information about your business or organization.

- Social media groups: Social media platforms like Facebook, LinkedIn, and Reddit have groups or communities that businesses and organizations can participate in as part of their forum marketing efforts. These groups can be helpful for connecting with a specific audience and for sharing information about your business or organization.

In conclusion, forum marketing is a powerful tool for attracting targeted traffic and building credibility and thought leadership. By actively participating in relevant forums and sharing valuable and relevant information, businesses and organizations can drive traffic to their website or online presence and establish themselves as thought leaders in their industry or niche. By finding and participating in relevant forums or discussion groups, tracking and analyzing your forum participation, and being mindful of ethical and legal considerations, you can effectively use forum marketing to attract targeted traffic and achieve your goals.

Chapter 13: Blogging for Driving Traffic and Engaging Readers

Blogging is a strategy that involves creating and sharing content on a regular basis, typically through a website or online platform, with the goal of driving traffic and engaging readers. By creating high-quality and informative content and promoting and distributing the content effectively, businesses and organizations can increase brand awareness, drive traffic to their website or online presence, and build a loyal and engaged audience. In this chapter, we will explore the various forms of blogging and discuss the benefits and considerations of using blogging for driving traffic and engaging readers.

One key aspect of blogging is creating high-quality and informative content. This involves developing a clear concept and message for the blog, and ensuring that the content is well-written, well-researched, and easy to read. It's also important to consider the format of the blog, as well as the target audience and the platform on which the blog will be shared.

Another important aspect of blogging is promoting and distributing the content. This can involve sharing the content on social media and other online platforms, as well as using paid advertising to reach a wider audience. It's also important to optimize the blog for search engines by including relevant keywords and tags, and to track and analyze the performance of the blog.

One of the key benefits of blogging is the ability to drive traffic to a website or online presence. By creating high-quality and informative content and promoting and distributing the content effectively, businesses and organizations can drive traffic to their website or online presence and increase visibility for their brand or organization.

Another benefit of blogging is the opportunity to engage and build a loyal audience. By consistently creating and sharing valuable and informative content, businesses and organizations can attract and retain a dedicated group of readers.

There are a few key considerations to keep in mind when using blogging to drive traffic and engage readers. One is the need to create high-quality and informative content. It's important to develop a clear concept and message for the blog, and to ensure that the content is well-written, well-researched, and easy to read. It's also important to consider the format of the blog, as well as the target audience and the platform on which the blog will be shared.

Another consideration is the need to effectively promote and distribute the content. This will involve sharing the content on social media and other online platforms, and using paid advertising to reach a wider audience. It's also important to optimize the blog for search engines and to track and analyze the performance of the blog.

In addition to these considerations, it's important to be mindful of ethical and legal considerations when using blogging. This can include ensuring that you have permission to use any images or music in the blog, and complying with relevant laws and regulations such as copyright laws.

There are several different types of blogs that businesses and organizations can create and share as part of their marketing efforts. Some common types of blogs include:

- Personal blogs: Personal blogs are blogs that are written by an individual and typically focus on personal experiences, opinions, and insights. These blogs can be helpful for building a personal brand and for sharing personal stories and experiences.
- Company blogs: Company blogs are blogs that are created and maintained by a business or organization. These blogs can be helpful for sharing company news, updates, and insights, and for building a company brand.
- Niche blogs: Niche blogs are blogs that are focused on a specific topic or theme, such as a particular industry or hobby. These blogs can be helpful for attracting a targeted audience and for sharing specialized knowledge and insights.
- Multi-author blogs: Multi-author blogs are blogs that are written by multiple authors and typically cover a wide range of topics. These blogs can be helpful for providing a range of

perspectives and for building a strong team brand.

In conclusion, blogging is a powerful tool for driving traffic and building a loyal and engaged audience. By creating high-quality and informative content and promoting and distributing the content effectively, businesses and organizations can increase brand awareness, drive traffic, and attract and retain a dedicated group of readers. By creating valuable and informative content, promoting and distributing the content effectively, and being mindful of ethical and legal considerations, you can effectively use blogging to drive traffic and engage readers and achieve your goals.

Chapter 14: Slideshare and Other Presentation Sharing Sites for Generating Traffic

Slideshare and other presentation sharing sites are platforms that allow users to upload and share presentations, infographics, and other visual content. By creating and sharing high-quality and informative visual content on these platforms, businesses and organizations can increase brand awareness, drive traffic to their website or online presence, and build an engaged and loyal audience. In this chapter, we will explore the various forms of presentation sharing sites and discuss the benefits and considerations of using these platforms for generating traffic.

One key aspect of using presentation sharing sites for traffic generation is creating high-quality and informative visual content. This involves developing a clear concept and message for the presentation, and ensuring that the content is well-designed and easy to understand. It's also important to consider the format of the presentation and the target audience, and to optimize the content for search engines by including relevant keywords and tags.

Another important aspect of using presentation sharing sites for traffic generation is promoting and distributing the content. This can involve sharing the content on social media and other online platforms, as well as using paid advertising to reach a wider audience. It's also important to track and analyze the performance of the content, and to engage with the audience by responding to comments and questions.

One of the key benefits of using presentation sharing sites for traffic generation is the ability to drive traffic to a website or online presence. By creating high-quality and informative visual content and promoting and distributing the content effectively, businesses and organizations can drive traffic to their website or online presence and increase visibility for their brand or organization.

Another benefit of using presentation sharing sites for traffic generation is the opportunity to build an engaged and loyal audience. By consistently creating and sharing valuable and informative visual content, businesses and organizations can attract and retain a dedicated group of viewers.

There are a few key considerations to keep in mind when using presentation sharing sites for traffic generation. One is the need to create high-quality and informative visual content. It's important to develop a clear concept and message for the presentation, and to ensure that the content is well-designed and easy to understand. It's also important to consider the format of the presentation and the target audience, and to optimize the content for search engines by including relevant keywords and tags.

Another consideration is the need to effectively promote and distribute the content. This will involve sharing the content on social media and other online platforms, and using paid advertising to reach a wider audience. It's also important to track and analyze the performance of the content, and to engage with the audience by responding to comments and questions.

In addition to these considerations, it's important to be mindful of ethical and legal

considerations when using presentation sharing sites for traffic generation. This can include ensuring that you have permission to use any images or music in the presentation, and complying with the terms of service of the presentation sharing platform.

There are several different types of presentation sharing sites that businesses and organizations can use as part of their marketing efforts. Some of the most popular presentation sharing sites includes:

- Slideshare: Slideshare is a platform owned by LinkedIn that allows users to upload and share presentations, infographics, and other visual content. It has a large user base and is a popular choice for businesses and organizations looking to share visual content.
- Prezi: Prezi is a cloud-based presentation platform that allows users to create and share interactive and visually appealing presentations. It offers a range of templates and design options and is popular for its unique and engaging presentation style.
- Google Slides: Google Slides is a presentation tool that is part of the Google Suite of productivity tools. It allows users to create and

share presentations online, and offers collaboration and real-time editing features.

In conclusion, presentation sharing sites are a powerful tool for generating traffic and building an engaged and loyal audience. By creating high-quality and informative visual content and promoting and distributing the content effectively, businesses and organizations can drive traffic to their website or online presence and attract and retain a dedicated group of viewers. By creating valuable and informative visual content, promoting and distributing the content effectively, and being mindful of ethical and legal considerations, you can effectively use presentation sharing sites for traffic generation and achieve your goals.

Chapter 15: Local SEO for Attracting Local Traffic to Your Business

Local SEO is a type of search engine optimization (SEO) that focuses on optimizing a business or organization's online presence to attract local traffic. By optimizing a website and other online profiles for local search terms and signals, businesses and organizations can increase visibility for their brand and attract local customers and clients. In this chapter, we will explore the various elements of local SEO and discuss the benefits and considerations of using local SEO to attract local traffic to your business.

One key element of local SEO is optimizing your website and other online profiles for local search terms and signals. This involves including relevant local keywords and phrases in your website content and meta tags, as well as ensuring that your website and online profiles are properly indexed and listed in local directories and business listings. Other important elements of local SEO include optimizing your website for mobile devices, and ensuring that your website and online profiles are up-to-date and accurate.

Another important element of local SEO is building and managing online reviews and ratings. By encouraging customers and clients to leave positive reviews and ratings on your website and online profiles, you can improve your local search rankings and build trust and credibility with local customers and clients. It's also important to respond to any negative reviews or ratings in a timely and professional manner.

One of the key benefits of using local SEO to attract local traffic to your business is the ability to increase visibility and attract local customers and clients. By optimizing your website and other online profiles for local search terms and signals, and by building and managing online reviews and ratings, you can increase visibility for your brand and attract local customers and clients.

Another benefit of using local SEO to attract local traffic to your business is the opportunity to build trust and credibility with local customers and clients. By consistently providing high-quality products and services and by actively managing your online reputation, you can build trust and credibility with local customers and clients.

There are a few key considerations to keep in mind when using local SEO to attract local traffic to your business. One is the need to optimize your website and other online profiles for local search terms and signals. This involves including relevant local keywords and phrases in your website content and meta tags, and ensuring that your website and online profiles are properly indexed and listed in local directories and business listings. It's also important to optimize your website for mobile devices, and to ensure that your website and online profiles are up-to-date and accurate.

Another consideration is the need to build and manage online reviews and ratings. By encouraging customers and clients to leave positive reviews and ratings on your website and online profiles, you can improve your local search rankings and build trust and credibility with local customers and clients. It's also important to respond to any negative reviews or ratings in a timely and professional manner.

In addition to these considerations, it's important to be mindful of ethical and legal considerations when using local SEO to attract local traffic to your business. This can include ensuring that you are compliant with any relevant laws and regulations, and that you are not engaging in any deceptive or misleading practices.

There are several different strategies and tactics that businesses and organizations can use as part of their local SEO efforts. Some of the most effective strategies and tactics include:

- Optimizing your website for local keywords and phrases: By including relevant local keywords and phrases in your website content and Meta tags, you can improve your local search rankings and attract local traffic.
- Claiming and optimizing your Google My Business listing: By claiming and optimizing your Google My Business listing, you can

improve your local search rankings and provide important information to local customers and clients, such as your business location, hours, and contact information.
- Building and managing online reviews and ratings: By encouraging customers and clients to leave positive reviews and ratings on your website and online profiles, you can improve your local search rankings and build trust and credibility with local customers and clients.
- Using local schema markup: By using local schema markup, you can help search engines understand the context and location of your website and improve your local search rankings.
- Using local business directories and listings: By including your business in local business directories and listings, you can improve your local search visibility and attract local traffic.

In conclusion, local SEO is a powerful tool for attracting local traffic to your business. By optimizing your website and other online profiles for local search terms and signals, and by building and managing online reviews and ratings, you can increase visibility for your brand and attract local customers and clients. By optimizing your website and online profiles for local search terms and signals, building and managing online reviews and ratings, and being mindful of ethical and legal considerations, you can effectively use local SEO to attract local traffic to your business and achieve your goals.

Chapter 16: International SEO for Attracting Global Traffic

International SEO is a type of search engine optimization (SEO) that focuses on optimizing a business or organization's online presence to attract global traffic. By optimizing a website and other online profiles for international search terms and signals, businesses and organizations can increase visibility for their brand and attract global customers and clients. In this chapter, we will explore the various elements of international SEO and discuss the benefits and considerations of using international SEO to attract global traffic.

One key element of international SEO is optimizing your website and other online profiles for international search terms and signals. This involves including relevant international keywords and phrases in your website content and meta tags, as well as ensuring that your website and online profiles are properly indexed and listed in international directories and business listings. Other important elements of international SEO include optimizing your website for mobile devices, and ensuring that your website and online profiles are up-to-date and accurate.

Another important element of international SEO is building and managing online reviews and ratings. By encouraging customers and clients to leave positive reviews and ratings on your website and online profiles, you can improve your international search rankings and build trust and credibility with global customers and clients. It's also important to respond to any negative reviews or ratings in a timely and professional manner.

One of the key benefits of using international SEO to attract global traffic is the ability to increase visibility and attract global customers and clients. By optimizing your website and other online profiles for international search terms and signals, and by building and managing online reviews and ratings, you can increase visibility for your brand and attract global customers and clients.

Another benefit of using international SEO to attract global traffic is the opportunity to build trust and credibility with global customers and clients. By consistently providing high-quality products and services and by actively managing your online reputation, you can build trust and credibility with global customers and clients.

There are a few key considerations to keep in mind when using international SEO to attract global traffic. One is the need to optimize your website and other online profiles for international search terms and signals. This involves including relevant international keywords and phrases in your website content and meta tags, and ensuring that your website and online profiles are properly indexed and listed in international directories and business listings. It's also important to optimize your website for mobile devices, and to ensure that your website and online profiles are up-to-date and accurate.

Another consideration is the need to build and manage online reviews and ratings. By encouraging customers and clients to leave positive reviews and ratings on your website and online profiles, you can improve your international search rankings and build trust and credibility with global customers and clients. It's also important to respond to any negative reviews or ratings in a timely and professional manner.

In addition to these considerations, it's important to be mindful of cultural and linguistic differences when using international SEO to attract global traffic. This includes adapting your website and marketing materials to the local language and customs of your target audience, and being aware of any cultural sensitivities or taboos.

There are several different strategies and tactics that businesses and organizations can use as part of their international SEO efforts. Some of the most effective strategies and tactics include:

- Optimizing your website for international keywords and phrases: By including relevant international keywords and phrases in your website content and Meta tags, you can improve your international search rankings and attract global traffic.

- Claiming and optimizing your Google My Business listing: By claiming and optimizing your Google My Business listing, you can improve your international search rankings and provide important information to global customers and clients, such as your business location, hours, and contact information.
- Building and managing online reviews and ratings: By encouraging customers and clients to leave positive reviews and ratings on your website and online profiles, you can improve your international search rankings and build trust and credibility with global customers and clients.
- Using international schema markup: By using international schema markup, you can help search engines understand the context and location of your website and improve your international search rankings.
- Using international business directories and listings: By including your business in international business directories and listings, you can improve your international search visibility and attract global traffic.

By implementing these and other strategies and tactics, businesses and organizations can effectively use international SEO to attract global traffic.

In conclusion, international SEO is a powerful tool for attracting global traffic. By optimizing your website and other online profiles for international search terms and signals, and by building and managing online reviews and ratings, you can increase visibility for your brand and attract global customers and clients. By optimizing your website and online profiles for international search terms and signals, building and managing online reviews and ratings, and being mindful of cultural and linguistic differences, you can effectively use international SEO to attract global traffic and achieve your goals.

Chapter 17:
E-commerce Traffic Strategies For Online Stores

E-commerce traffic strategies are a set of tactics and strategies that businesses and organizations can use to drive traffic to their online stores and increase sales. In this chapter, we will explore the various e-commerce traffic strategies that businesses and organizations can use to attract visitors to their online stores and convert them into paying customers.

One key e-commerce traffic strategy is search engine optimization (SEO). By optimizing your online store and product pages for relevant keywords and phrases, you can increase visibility in search engines and attract visitors to your online store. This can include optimizing your website and product pages for on-page SEO factors, such as title tags, meta descriptions, and headings, as well as building high-quality back links to your website.

Another effective e-commerce traffic strategy is paid advertising. By using platforms like Google

AdWords, Facebook Ads, and Instagram Ads, you can target specific audiences and drive traffic to your online store. Paid advertising can be an effective way to quickly drive traffic to your online store and generate sales, but it can also be costly if not managed properly.

Content marketing is another e-commerce traffic strategy that can be effective for driving traffic to your online store. By creating and sharing valuable, informative, and engaging content on your blog, social media channels, and other platforms, you can attract visitors to your online store and build trust and credibility with potential customers.

Social media marketing is another e-commerce traffic strategy that can be effective for driving traffic to your online store. By actively participating in social media platforms, such as Facebook, Twitter, and Instagram, and by creating and sharing engaging and relevant content, you can attract visitors to your online store and build a community of loyal customers.

Email marketing is another e-commerce traffic strategy that can be effective for driving traffic to your online store. By building and maintaining an email list of subscribers and by sending targeted and personalized email campaigns, you can encourage visitors to visit your online store and make a purchase.

Affiliate marketing is another e-commerce traffic strategy that can be effective for driving traffic to your online store. By partnering with other websites and bloggers and by offering them a commission for promoting your products, you can drive traffic to your online store and generate sales.

Another e-commerce traffic strategy is to offer special promotions and discounts to attract visitors to your online store. This can include offering discounts to first-time customers, offering free shipping or returns, or offering limited-time promotions and sales.

Another strategy is to optimize your website and online store for mobile devices. With the increasing prevalence of mobile devices, it's important to ensure that your online store is optimized for mobile devices in order to attract and retain mobile visitors.

Another strategy is to focus on customer experience. By providing a seamless and enjoyable shopping experience for your customers, you can increase the likelihood that they will return to your online store in the future. This can include offering a user-friendly website, providing clear product descriptions and images, and offering multiple payment and shipping options.

Finally, it's important to track and analyze your traffic and sales data in order to understand what's working and what's not. By using tools like Google Analytics, you can track key metrics such as website traffic, conversion rates, and sales, and use this data to make informed decisions about your e-commerce traffic strategies.

In conclusion, there are several different e-commerce traffic strategies that businesses and organizations can use to drive traffic to their online stores and increase sales. These strategies include search engine optimization (SEO), paid advertising, content marketing, social media marketing, email marketing, affiliate marketing, offering promotions and discounts, optimizing for mobile devices, focusing on customer experience, and tracking and analyzing traffic and sales data. By implementing a combination of these strategies, businesses and organizations can effectively drive traffic to their online stores and achieve their goals.

In conclusion, there are several different e-commerce traffic strategies that businesses and organizations can use to drive traffic to their online stores and increase sales. These strategies include search engine optimization (SEO), paid advertising, content marketing, social media marketing, email marketing, and affiliate marketing. By implementing a combination of these strategies, businesses and organizations can effectively drive traffic to their online store.

Chapter 18: Mobile Marketing for Reaching Mobile Users

Mobile marketing is a type of marketing that specifically targets mobile device users. In this chapter, we will explore the various tactics and strategies that businesses and organizations can use as part of their mobile marketing efforts to reach and engage mobile users.

One key element of mobile marketing is having a mobile-friendly website. With the increasing prevalence of mobile devices, it's important to ensure that your website is optimized for mobile devices in order to attract and retain mobile visitors. This can include using a responsive design, reducing page load times, and ensuring that all content and functionality is easily accessible on mobile devices.

Another important element of mobile marketing is SMS marketing. By sending targeted text messages to mobile users, businesses and organizations can communicate directly with their audience and drive traffic to their website or online store. SMS marketing can be an effective way to reach mobile users, but it's important to ensure that you have permission to send texts and to follow best practices in order to avoid spamming or annoying your audience.

Mobile apps can also be an effective part of a mobile marketing strategy. By developing a mobile app, businesses and organizations can provide a convenient and engaging way for mobile users to interact with their brand. Mobile apps can include a range of features, such as push notifications, location-based services, and in-app purchasing, and can be a powerful way to reach and engage mobile users.

Mobile advertising is another important element of mobile marketing. By using platforms like Google Ad Words, Facebook Ads, and Instagram Ads, businesses and organizations can target specific mobile users with targeted and personalized ads. Mobile advertising can be an effective way to reach and engage mobile users, but it's important to carefully target and optimize your ads in order to maximize your return on investment.

Mobile marketing can also include the use of mobile messaging apps like WhatsApp, WeChat, and Facebook Messenger to communicate with and engage mobile users. These messaging apps allow businesses and organizations to send messages directly to their audience and can be an effective way to reach and engage mobile users.

Location-based marketing is another important element of mobile marketing. By using location-based services like GPS, businesses and organizations can target mobile users with relevant and personalized messages based on their location. For example, a business could send a promotion to users who are within a certain radius of their physical location.

Mobile video marketing is another tactic that businesses and organizations can use as part of their mobile marketing efforts. By creating and sharing engaging and relevant video content on platforms like YouTube, Facebook, and Instagram, businesses and organizations can reach and engage mobile users and drive traffic to their website or online store.

In-game advertising is another mobile marketing tactic that businesses and organizations can use to reach mobile users. By placing ads within mobile games, businesses and organizations can reach a specific and engaged audience and drive traffic to their website or online store.

Finally, mobile influencer marketing is a tactic that businesses and organizations can use to reach and engage mobile users. By partnering with influencers who have a large and engaged following on mobile platforms, businesses and organizations can reach and engage a targeted audience and drive traffic to their website or online store.

In conclusion, there are several different tactics and strategies that businesses and organizations can use as part of their mobile marketing efforts to reach and engage mobile users. These tactics include having a mobile-friendly website, using SMS marketing, developing mobile apps, using mobile advertising, using mobile messaging apps, utilizing location-based marketing, creating mobile video content, using in-game advertising, and partnering with mobile influencers. By implementing a combination of these tactics, businesses and organizations can effectively reach and engage mobile users and achieve their goals.

Chapter 19: App Marketing for Driving Traffic to Mobile Apps

App marketing is a type of marketing that specifically focuses on driving traffic and engagement to mobile apps. In this chapter, we will explore the various tactics and strategies that businesses and organizations can use as part of their app marketing efforts.

One key element of app marketing is optimizing your app for app store search. By including relevant keywords and phrases in your app's title and description and by using visually appealing and high-quality app screenshots and videos, you can improve your app's visibility in app stores and increase the likelihood that it will be downloaded by users.

Another important element of app marketing is using paid advertising to drive traffic to your app. By using platforms like Google Ad Words, Facebook Ads, and Instagram Ads, you can target specific audiences and drive traffic to your app. Paid advertising can be an effective way to quickly drive traffic to your app, but it's important to carefully target and optimize your ads in order to maximize your return on investment.

Content marketing is another tactic that businesses and organizations can use as part of their app marketing efforts. By creating and sharing valuable, informative, and engaging content on your blog, social media channels, and other platforms, you can attract users to your app and build trust and credibility with potential customers.

Social media marketing is another tactic that businesses and organizations can use to drive traffic to their app. By actively participating in social media platforms, such as Facebook, Twitter, and Instagram, and by creating and sharing engaging and relevant content, you can attract users to your app and build a community of loyal customers.

Email marketing is another tactic that businesses and organizations can use to drive traffic to their app. By building and maintaining an email list of subscribers and by sending targeted and personalized email campaigns, you can encourage users to download your app and engage with it.

App store optimization (ASO) is another important element of app marketing. Similar to search engine optimization (SEO) for websites, ASO involves optimizing your app's listing in app stores in order to improve its visibility and increase the likelihood that it will be downloaded by users. This can include optimizing your app's title, description, keywords, and visuals, as well as encouraging users to leave reviews and ratings.

Another tactic that businesses and organizations can use as part of their app marketing efforts is influencer marketing. By partnering with influencers who have a large and engaged following on social media or other platforms, businesses and organizations can reach and engage a targeted audience and drive traffic to their app.

Another tactic that businesses and organizations can use is cross-promotion. By partnering with other businesses or organizations and promoting each other's apps, you can drive traffic to your app and increase its visibility.

Another tactic that businesses and organizations can use is offering incentives or rewards to users who download and engage with their app. This can include offering discounts, exclusive content, or other perks to encourage users to download and use your app.

Finally, it's important to track and analyze your app's performance in order to understand what's working and what's not. By using tools like Google Analytics, you can track key metrics such as app downloads, user retention, and in-app purchases, and use this data to inform your app marketing efforts.

Another tactic that businesses and organizations can use as part of their app marketing efforts is app localization. By localizing your app and its marketing materials into different languages and cultural contexts, you can reach and engage a global audience and drive traffic to your app.

Another tactic that businesses and organizations can use is app indexing. By indexing your app in search engines, you can improve its visibility and make it easier for users to find and download your app.

Another tactic that businesses and organizations can use is app deep linking. By using deep links, you can direct users to specific pages or content within your app from external sources, such as social media or email campaigns. This can be an effective way to drive traffic to your app and increase engagement.

Another tactic that businesses and organizations can use is app re-engagement. By sending targeted and personalized messages to users who have downloaded your app but have not used it recently, you can encourage them to re-engage with your app and drive traffic to it.

Finally, another tactic that businesses and organizations can use as part of their app marketing efforts is app partnerships and collaborations. By partnering with other businesses or organizations and promoting each other's apps, you can drive traffic to your app and increase its visibility.

In conclusion, there are several different tactics and strategies that businesses and organizations can use as part of their app marketing efforts. These tactics include app store optimization (ASO), influencer marketing, and cross-promotion, offering incentives and rewards, and tracking and analyzing app performance. By implementing a combination of these tactics, businesses and organizations can effectively drive traffic to their app and achieve their goals.

Chapter 20:
Online Public Relations for Generating Traffic and Building Visibility

Online public relations (PR) is a type of marketing that focuses on building and maintaining a positive image and reputation for a business or organization online. In this chapter, we will explore the various tactics and strategies that businesses and organizations can use as part of their online PR efforts to generate traffic and build visibility.

One key element of online PR is having a strong and well-designed website. By having a visually appealing and user-friendly website, businesses and organizations can attract visitors and establish credibility with their audience.

Another important element of online PR is building and maintaining a presence on social media. By actively participating in social media platforms, such as Facebook, Twitter, and Instagram, and by creating and sharing engaging and relevant content, businesses and organizations can build a community of loyal followers and attract new visitors to their website.

Content marketing is another tactic that businesses and organizations can use as part of their online PR efforts. By creating and sharing valuable, informative, and engaging content on their blog, social media channels, and other platforms, businesses and organizations can attract visitors to their website and build trust and credibility with their audience.

Online media relations are another important element of online PR. By building relationships with online journalists and bloggers and by pitching relevant and newsworthy stories, businesses and organizations can secure coverage in online media outlets and drive traffic to their website.

Another tactic that businesses and organizations can use as part of their online PR efforts is influencer marketing. By partnering with influencers who have a large and engaged following on social media or other platforms, businesses and organizations can reach and engage a targeted audience and drive traffic to their website.

Another tactic that businesses and organizations can use is online events and webinars. By hosting online events and webinars, businesses and organizations can attract visitors to their website and build their reputation as thought leaders in their industry.

Another tactic that businesses and organizations can use is online reputation management. By monitoring and managing their online reputation, businesses and organizations can ensure that their brand is being presented in a positive light and address any negative feedback or criticism in a timely and effective manner.

It's important to track and analyze the performance of your online PR efforts in order to understand what's working and what's not. By using tools like Google Analytics, you can track key metrics such as website traffic, social media engagement, and media mentions, and use this data to inform your online PR strategy.

One tactic that businesses and organizations can use to improve their online PR efforts is by optimizing their website for search engines. By including relevant keywords and phrases in the content and meta data of their website, businesses and organizations can improve the visibility of their website in search engine results pages (SERPs) and attract more organic traffic.

Another tactic that businesses and organizations can use is by actively participating in online communities and forums related to their industry. By contributing valuable insights and engaging with other members, businesses and organizations can build their reputation as thought leaders and attract visitors to their website.

Guest blogging is another tactic that businesses and organizations can use as part of their online PR efforts. By writing and publishing guest posts on other websites and blogs in their industry, businesses and organizations can build their credibility, reach a new audience, and drive traffic to their website.

Another tactic that businesses and organizations can use is by leveraging their existing customer base and encouraging them to share their website and content on social media and other platforms. By providing incentives and rewards to customers who share their content, businesses and organizations can increase their reach and attract new visitors to their website.

In conclusion, there are several different tactics and strategies that businesses and organizations can use as part of their online PR efforts. These tactics include having a strong and well-designed website, building and maintaining a presence on social media, creating and sharing content, and engaging in online media relations. By implementing a combination of these tactics, businesses and organizations can effectively generate traffic and build visibility online and achieve their goals.

Chapter 21: Online Reputation Management for Protecting and Enhancing Traffic

Online reputation management is the process of monitoring and managing the reputation of a business or organization online. In this chapter, we will explore the various tactics and strategies that businesses and organizations can use as part of their online reputation management efforts to protect and enhance traffic.

One key element of online reputation management is monitoring and tracking your online reputation. By using tools like Google Alerts, businesses and organizations can track mentions of their brand online and be notified of any new content that is published about them. This allows them to quickly identify and address any negative feedback or criticism that may be impacting their reputation.

Another important element of online reputation management is responding to negative feedback and criticism. By addressing negative feedback and criticism in a timely and professional manner, businesses and organizations can mitigate the impact on their reputation and show their customers that they care about their concerns.

Content marketing is another tactic that businesses and organizations can use as part of their online reputation management efforts. By creating and sharing valuable, informative, and engaging content on their blog, social media channels, and other platforms, businesses and organizations can attract visitors to their website and build trust and credibility with their audience.

Online media relations are another tactic that businesses and organizations can use as part of their online reputation management efforts. By building relationships with online journalists and bloggers and by pitching relevant and newsworthy stories, businesses and organizations can secure coverage in online media outlets and improve their reputation.

Another tactic that businesses and organizations can use is by leveraging their existing customer base and encouraging them to share positive reviews and feedback about their brand on social media and other platforms. This can help to counteract any negative feedback or criticism and improve the overall perception of their brand.

Finally, it's important to track and analyze the performance of your online reputation management efforts in order to understand what's working and what's not. By using tools like Google Analytics, you can track key metrics such as website traffic, social media engagement, and media mentions, and use this data to inform your online reputation management strategy.

In conclusion, there are several different tactics and strategies that businesses and organizations can use as part of their online reputation management efforts. These tactics include influencer marketing, participating in online communities and forums, guest blogging, leveraging their customer base, and tracking and analyzing performance. By implementing a combination of these tactics, businesses and organizations can effectively protect and enhance their online reputation and traffic.

Chapter 22: Web Design and User Experience for Boosting Traffic and Conversions

Web design and user experience (UX) refer to the look, feel, and overall experience of a website. In this chapter, we will explore the various tactics and strategies that businesses and organizations can use as part of their web design and UX efforts to boost traffic and conversions.

One key element of web design and UX is having a visually appealing and user-friendly website. By using a clean and modern design, using high-quality images and graphics, and organizing content in a logical and easy-to-navigate manner, businesses and organizations can attract visitors to their website and improve the overall user experience.

Another important element of web design and UX is mobile-friendliness. With the increasing number of users accessing the internet on their smartphones and tablets, it's important for businesses and organizations to ensure that their website is optimized for mobile devices. This includes using responsive design techniques that ensure that the website layout and content adjusts to fit the screen size of the device it is being viewed on.

Content marketing is another tactic that businesses and organizations can use as part of their web design and UX efforts. By creating and sharing valuable, informative, and engaging content on their blog, social media channels, and other platforms, businesses and organizations can attract visitors to their website and improve the user experience.

It's important to track and analyze the performance of your website in order to understand what's working and what's not. By using tools like Google Analytics, you can track key metrics such as website traffic, bounce rate, and conversion rate, and use this data to inform your web design and UX strategy.

Another tactic that businesses and organizations can use as part of their web design and UX efforts is by using calls-to-action (CTAs) strategically throughout their website.

CTAs are buttons or links that encourage visitors to take a specific action, such as signing up for a newsletter, making a purchase, or filling out a form. By using compelling and clear CTAs, businesses and organizations can increase conversions and achieve their goals.

Another tactic that businesses and organizations can use is by optimizing the loading speed of their website. Users are more likely to leave a website if it takes too long to load, so it's important for businesses and organizations to optimize the loading speed of their website in order to improve the user experience and increase conversions.

Another tactic that businesses and organizations can use is by conducting user testing and gathering feedback from their audience. By asking users to complete tasks on their website and gathering feedback on their experience, businesses and organizations can identify areas for improvement and optimize the user experience.

Businesses and organizations can use A/B testing to optimize their website and improve the user experience. A/B testing involves creating two versions of a website or a specific element of a website, such as a CTA, and testing which version performs better in terms of conversions or other desired outcomes. By conducting A/B tests, businesses and organizations can identify the best version and make informed decisions about their web design and UX strategy.

Another tactic that businesses and organizations can use as part of their web design and UX efforts is by using personalized and targeted messaging. By using data and insights about their audience, businesses and organizations can create personalized and targeted messaging that resonates with their target audience and improves the user experience.

Another tactic that businesses and organizations can use is by incorporating social proof, such as customer reviews and testimonials, into their website design. Social proof can help to build trust and credibility with visitors and increase conversions.

Another tactic that businesses and organizations can use is by using clear and concise copy that is easy to read and understand. By using simple language and formatting techniques such as bullet points and headings, businesses and organizations can improve the user experience and increase conversions.

Finally, businesses and organizations can use storytelling as part of their web design and UX efforts. By incorporating storytelling elements, such as storytelling through images and video, businesses and organizations can engage their audience and improve the user experience.

In conclusion, there are several different tactics and strategies that businesses and organizations can use as part of their web design and UX efforts. These tactics include having a visually appealing and user-friendly website, mobile-friendliness, creating and sharing content, and tracking and analyzing performance. By implementing a combination of these tactics, businesses and organizations can effectively boost traffic and conversions on their website and achieve their goals.

Chapter 23: Conversion Optimization for Turning Traffic into Customers

Conversion optimization is the process of improving the performance of a website in terms of turning visitors into customers or achieving other desired outcomes. In this chapter, we will explore the various tactics and strategies that businesses and organizations can use as part of their conversion optimization efforts.

One key element of conversion optimization is having a clear and compelling value proposition. A value proposition is a statement that clearly communicates the benefits and value that a business or organization offers to its customers. By having a clear and compelling value proposition, businesses and organizations can attract visitors to their website and improve the chances of converting them into customers.

Another important element of conversion optimization is having a user-friendly and easy-to-navigate website. By organizing content in a logical and easy-to-navigate manner and using clear and compelling calls-to-action (CTAs), businesses and organizations can improve the chances of converting visitors into customers.

Content marketing is another tactic that businesses and organizations can use as part of their conversion optimization efforts. By creating and sharing valuable, informative, and engaging content on their blog, social media channels, and other platforms, businesses and organizations can attract visitors to their website and improve the chances of converting them into customers.

It's important to track and analyze the performance of your website in order to understand what's working and what's not. By using tools like Google Analytics, you can track key metrics such as website traffic, bounce rate, and conversion rate, and use this data to inform your conversion optimization strategy.

Another tactic that businesses and organizations can use as part of their conversion optimization efforts is by using targeted and personalized messaging. By using data and insights about their audience, businesses and organizations can create targeted and personalized messaging that resonates with their target audience and improves the chances of converting them into customers.

Another tactic that businesses and organizations can use is by using social proof, such as customer reviews and testimonials, to build trust and credibility with visitors. By showcasing the positive experiences of other customers, businesses and organizations can improve the chances of converting visitors into customers.

Another tactic that businesses and organizations can use is by optimizing the loading speed of their website. Users are more likely to leave a website if it takes too long to load, so it's important for businesses and organizations to optimize the loading speed of their website in order to improve the user experience and increase conversions.

Businesses and organizations can use A/B testing to optimize their website and improve the chances of converting visitors into customers. A/B testing involves creating two versions of a website or a specific element of a website, such as a CTA, and testing which version performs better in terms of conversions or other desired outcomes. By conducting A/B tests, businesses and organizations can identify the best version and make informed decisions about their conversion optimization strategy.

Another tactic that businesses and organizations can use as part of their conversion optimization efforts is by leveraging the power of scarcity and urgency. By highlighting limited time offers, limited quantities, or other types of scarcity and urgency, businesses and organizations can create a sense of urgency in the minds of visitors and improve the chances of converting them into customers.

Another tactic that businesses and organizations can use is by using clear and concise copy that is easy to read and understand. By using simple language and formatting techniques such as bullet points and headings, businesses and organizations can improve the user experience and increase conversions.

Another tactic that businesses and organizations can use is by using video marketing to showcase their products or services and improve the chances of converting visitors into customers. By using video to demonstrate the benefits and features of their products or services, businesses and organizations can engage and persuade visitors in a more effective way than with text alone.

Businesses and organizations can use personalization as part of their conversion optimization efforts. By using data and insights about their audience, businesses and organizations can create personalized experiences for visitors and improve the chances of converting them into customers.

Another tactic that businesses and organizations can use as part of their conversion optimization efforts is by using retargeting to bring visitors back to their website. Retargeting involves showing targeted ads to visitors who have previously visited a website in an attempt to bring them back and convert them into customers. By using retargeting, businesses and organizations can improve the chances of converting visitors who may have left their website without taking any action.

Another tactic that businesses and organizations can use is by using live chat and other forms of customer support to assist visitors in real-time and improve the chances of converting them into customers. By providing prompt and helpful support, businesses and organizations can improve the user experience and increase conversions.

Another tactic that businesses and organizations can use is by using customer data and insights to improve the user experience and increase conversions. By using tools such as customer relationship management (CRM) systems and analytics, businesses and organizations can gather data and insights about their audience and use this information to optimize their website and improve the chances of converting visitors into customers.

Businesses and organizations can use social media marketing as part of their conversion optimization efforts. By using social media to promote their products or services and engage with their audience, businesses and organizations can attract visitors to their website and improve the chances of converting them into customers.

Another tactic that businesses and organizations can use as part of their conversion optimization efforts is by using persuasive design techniques. Persuasive design is the use of psychological principles and techniques to influence the behavior of website visitors and improve the chances of converting them into customers. Some common persuasive design techniques include using social proof, such as customer reviews and testimonials, to build trust and credibility with visitors; using scarcity and urgency to create a sense of urgency in the minds of visitors; and using personalization to create personalized experiences for visitors.

Another tactic that businesses and organizations can use is by using pop-ups and overlays to promote special offers, discounts, or other types of incentives to visitors. By using pop-ups and overlays in a targeted and non-intrusive way, businesses and organizations can improve the chances of converting visitors into customers.

Another tactic that businesses and organizations can use is by using chat bots to provide instant customer support and assistance to visitors. By using chat bots, businesses and organizations can provide prompt and helpful support to visitors and improve the chances of converting them into customers.

Finally, businesses and organizations can use customer journey mapping as part of their conversion optimization efforts. Customer journey mapping involves understanding the different steps that a customer goes through from awareness to purchase and identifying opportunities to optimize the customer experience and increase conversions.

In conclusion, there are several different tactics and strategies that businesses and organizations can use as part of their conversion optimization efforts. These tactics include having a clear and compelling value proposition, having a user-friendly and easy-to-navigate website, creating and sharing content, and tracking and analyzing performance. By implementing a combination of these tactics, <u>businesses and organizations can effectively turn traffic into customers and achieve their goals.</u>

Chapter 24:
Analyzing and Improving Your Online Traffic Mix

In order to analyze and improve your online traffic mix, it's important to first understand the different types of traffic that you are receiving. There are several different types of traffic that businesses and organizations can receive, including organic traffic, referral traffic, direct traffic, and paid traffic.

Organic traffic refers to visitors who arrive at a website through search engine results. This type of traffic is considered highly valuable because it is typically more targeted and engaged than other types of traffic.

Referral traffic refers to visitors who arrive at a website through links from other websites. This type of traffic can be valuable if it is coming from high-quality and relevant websites.

Direct traffic refers to visitors who arrive at a website by directly typing the URL into their browser or by clicking on a bookmark. This type of traffic can be valuable if it is coming from repeat visitors or brand advocates.

Paid traffic refers to visitors who arrive at a website through paid advertising efforts, such as pay-per-click (PPC) ads or sponsored content. This type of traffic can be valuable if it is targeted and results in conversions.

Once you have a good understanding of the different types of traffic that you are receiving, you can begin to analyze and improve your online traffic mix. Here are a few strategies that you can use:

1. Improve your search engine optimization (SEO) efforts: By optimizing your website and content for relevant keywords, you can improve your organic traffic and attract more targeted and engaged visitors.
2. Build back links from high-quality and relevant websites: By building back links from high-quality and relevant websites, you can improve your referral traffic and attract visitors who are interested in your products or services.
3. Invest in paid advertising: By investing in paid advertising efforts such as PPC ads, you can

attract targeted and engaged visitors who are interested in your products or services.
4. Analyze and optimize your website: By analyzing your website performance and user experience, you can identify areas for improvement and optimize your website to attract and convert more visitors.

Another strategy for analyzing and improving your online traffic mix is to use tracking and analysis tools to gather data about your visitors and their behavior. By using tools such as Google Analytics, you can track key metrics such as website traffic, bounce rate, and conversion rate and use this data to inform your strategy.

Another strategy is to segment your traffic and analyze the performance of different segments. By segmenting your traffic, you can identify patterns and trends that can help you understand the needs and preferences of different groups of visitors.

Another strategy is to conduct user testing and gather feedback from your visitors. By conducting user testing, you can identify issues and opportunities for improvement and optimize your website to better meet the needs and expectations of your visitors.

Finally, another strategy is to regularly review and update your online marketing strategy. By reviewing and updating your online marketing strategy on a regular basis, you can ensure that you are using the most effective tactics and strategies to attract and convert visitors.

In conclusion, analyzing and improving your online traffic mix involves understanding the different types of traffic that you are receiving and implementing strategies to attract and convert more targeted and engaged visitors. By following these strategies, you can improve the performance of your website and achieve your goals.

Chapter 25: Advanced Strategies for Maximizing Your Online Traffic Potential

There are several advanced strategies that businesses and organizations can use to maximize their online traffic potential. One strategy is to use content marketing to attract and engage visitors. Content marketing involves creating and sharing valuable, relevant, and consistent content to attract and retain a clearly defined audience. By using content marketing, businesses and organizations can attract visitors who are interested in their products or services and improve the chances of converting them into customers.

Another advanced strategy is to use influencer marketing to tap into the influence and reach of industry experts and influencers. By partnering with influencers and leveraging their audience, businesses and organizations can attract a large number of targeted and engaged visitors and improve their online traffic potential.

Another advanced strategy is to use social media marketing to reach and engage with a large and diverse audience. By using social media platforms such as Facebook, Twitter, and Instagram, businesses and organizations can attract and engage with visitors who are interested in their products or services and improve their online traffic potential.

Another advanced strategy is to use paid advertising to target and reach specific groups of visitors. By using paid advertising platforms such as Google Ad Words, businesses and organizations can target their ads to specific groups of visitors based on their interests and demographics and improve their online traffic potential.

Another advanced strategy is to use conversion rate optimization (CRO) to improve the performance of your website and increase conversions. By using CRO techniques such as A/B testing, businesses and organizations can optimize the design and functionality of their website and improve the chances of converting visitors into customers.

Another advanced strategy for maximizing your online traffic potential is to use data and analytics to inform your marketing decisions. By using tools such as Google Analytics, businesses and organizations can gather data about their website traffic and visitor behavior and use this data to inform their marketing strategy. By analyzing data such as traffic sources, landing pages, and conversion rates, businesses and organizations can identify opportunities for improvement and optimize their marketing efforts to attract and convert more visitors.

Another advanced strategy is to use personalization to create personalized experiences for visitors. By using customer data and insights, businesses and organizations can create personalized experiences for visitors based on their interests and preferences and improve the chances of converting them into customers.

Another advanced strategy is to use retargeting to bring visitors back to your website. Retargeting involves showing targeted ads to visitors who have previously visited your website in an attempt to bring them back and convert them into customers. By using retargeting, businesses and organizations can improve the chances of converting visitors who may have left their website without taking any action.

Another advanced strategy is to use video marketing to showcase your products or services and improve the chances of converting visitors into customers. By using video to demonstrate the benefits and features of your products or services, businesses and organizations can engage and persuade visitors in a more effective way than with text alone.

Another advanced strategy is to use chatbots and other forms of automated customer support to assist visitors in real-time and improve the chances of converting them into customers. By using chatbots, businesses and organizations can provide prompt and helpful support to visitors and improve the user experience.

Another advanced strategy for maximizing your online traffic potential is to use artificial intelligence (AI) and machine learning (ML) to optimize your marketing efforts. By using AI and ML, businesses and organizations can analyze large amounts of data and identify patterns and trends that can inform their marketing strategy. For example, businesses and organizations can use AI and ML to optimize their paid advertising efforts by identifying the most effective ad targeting and messaging strategies.

Another advanced strategy is to use customer relationship management (CRM) systems to manage and analyze customer data and insights. By using CRM systems, businesses and organizations can collect and store customer data such as contact information, purchase history, and preferences and use this data to inform their marketing efforts.

Another advanced strategy is to use customer data platforms (CDPs) to collect and store customer data from multiple sources and create a comprehensive view of the customer. By using CDPs, businesses and organizations can improve their understanding of their customers and create more targeted and personalized marketing campaigns.

Another advanced strategy is to use predictive analytics to forecast future customer behavior and inform marketing efforts. By using predictive analytics, businesses and organizations can identify potential customers and target their marketing efforts accordingly.

Finally, another advanced strategy is to use marketing automation to streamline and optimize marketing processes. By using marketing automation, businesses and organizations can automate tasks such as email marketing, social media marketing, and lead generation and improve the efficiency and effectiveness of their marketing efforts.

Another advanced strategy for maximizing your online traffic potential is to use voice search optimization to improve your visibility on voice search platforms such as Amazon Alexa and Google Home. By optimizing your website and content for voice search, businesses and organizations can improve their chances of being found by users who are using voice search to find information, products, or services.

Another advanced strategy is to use augmented reality (AR) and virtual reality (VR) to engage and persuade visitors. By using AR and VR, businesses and organizations can create immersive and interactive experiences for visitors and improve the chances of converting them into customers.

Another advanced strategy is to use conversational marketing to engage and persuade visitors in real-time. By using chatbots and other conversational marketing tools, businesses and organizations can provide personalized and timely support to visitors and improve the chances of converting them into customers.

Another advanced strategy is to use artificial intelligence (AI) and machine learning (ML) to optimize your website and improve the user experience. By using AI and ML, businesses and organizations can optimize the design and functionality of their website and improve the chances of converting visitors into customers.

Finally, another advanced strategy is to use data-driven design to optimize the look and feel of your website. By using data-driven design, businesses and organizations can create visually appealing and user-friendly websites that improve the chances of converting visitors into customers.

In conclusion, there are several advanced strategies that businesses and organizations can use to maximize their online traffic potential. These strategies include using voice search optimization, AR and VR, conversational marketing, AI and ML, and data-driven design. By implementing a combination of these strategies, businesses and organizations can attract and convert a large number of targeted and engaged visitors and achieve their goals.

www.ingramcontent.com/pod-product-compliance
Lightning Source LLC
Chambersburg PA
CBHW050002230526
45465CB00003BB/1227